I0426182

Baseline Plant Community Monitoring Report, Tallgrass Prairie National Preserve

Natural Resource Report NPS/HTLN/NRTR—2006/019
NPS D-33

Alicia Sasseen
National Park Service, The Heartland I&M Network and Prairie Cluster Prototype Monitoring Program
Wilson's Creek National Battlefield, 6424 West Farm Road 182, Republic, MO 65738

Mike DeBacker
National Park Service, The Heartland I&M Network and Prairie Cluster Prototype Monitoring Program
Wilson's Creek National Battlefield, 6424 West Farm Road 182, Republic, MO 65738

Heartland Network
Natural Resource Monitoring

April 2006

U.S. Department of the Interior
National Park Service
Natural Resource Program Center
Fort Collins, Colorado

The Natural Resource Publication series addresses natural resource topics that are of interest and applicability to a broad readership in the National Park Service and to others in the management of natural resources, including the scientific community, the public, and the NPS conservation and environmental constituencies. Manuscripts are peer-reviewed to ensure that the information is scientifically credible, technically accurate, appropriately written for the intended audience, and is designed and published in a professional manner.

The Natural Resource Technical Report series is used to disseminate the peer-reviewed results of scientific studies in the physical, biological, and social sciences for both the advancement of science and the achievement of the National Park Service's mission. The reports provide contributors with a forum for displaying comprehensive data that are often deleted from journals because of page limitations. Current examples of such reports include the results of research that addresses natural resource management issues; natural resource inventory and monitoring activities; resource assessment reports; scientific literature reviews; and peer reviewed proceedings of technical workshops, conferences, or symposia.

Views, statements, findings, conclusions, recommendations and data in this report are solely those of the author(s) and do not necessarily reflect views and policies of the U.S. Department of the Interior, NPS. Mention of trade names or commercial products does not constitute endorsement or recommendation for use by the National Park Service.

Printed copies of reports in these series may be produced in a limited quantity and they are only available as long as the supply lasts. This report is also available from the Heartland I&M Network website (http://www.nature.nps.gov/im/units/HTLN) on the internet, or by sending a request to the address on the back cover.

Please cite this publication as:

Sasseen, A., and DeBacker, M. 2006. Baseline Plant Community Monitoring Report, Tallgrass Prairie National Preserve. Natural Resource Technical Report NPS/HTLN/NRTR—2006/019. National Park Service, Fort Collins, Colorado.

NPS D-33, April 2006

Table of Contents

Figures

Tables

Introduction

The tallgrass prairie ecosystem once spread across more than 60 million hectares and extended from southern Texas to southern Manitoba (Collins and Glenn 1998). Now, however, it is estimated that as little as 1-4% (0.6-2.4 million ha) of the original tallgrass prairie remains (Weaver 1954). In addition to being highly fragmented and disparate, tallgrass prairie remnants tend to occur on sites of marginal agricultural use, usually steep slopes with rocky soils.

Historically, native tallgrass prairie was characterized by heterogeneity, with vegetation communities occurring in a patchwork of various conditions. The interaction of fire, grazing and climate formed a landscape in which few patches were burned or grazed at the same time or intensity every year (Hiebert 1998). It is estimated, using time until tree invasion under fire suppression, that historic grassland fire return intervals ranged from 3 to 5 years (Collins and Glenn 1995). In general, fires were relatively small in size (NPS 2000) and occurred in all seasons (Bragg 1995). Variability in fire frequency and size led to spatially variable grazing as native ungulates preferentially grazed newly burned patches. Non-grazing behaviors, such as wallowing, also increased landscape heterogeneity (Plumb and Dodd 1993).

The interaction of fire, grazing and climate affect ground flora composition and abundance in any given year (Albertson et al. 1957, Hartnett et al. 1996), often-making tallgrass prairies difficult communities to manage. However, the complexity of these ecosystems creates the potential for high biodiversity.

Tallgrass Prairie National Preserve (TAPR) is the first National Park Service area established specifically for the preservation, protection and interpretation of the tallgrass prairie ecosystem (Hiebert 1998). Formerly known as the Spring Hill Ranch area and continuously grazed for cattle production for over 120 years, TAPR consists of more than 9,000 acres of unplowed tallgrass prairie in the Flint Hills physiognomic province of Kansas. Land management of TAPR, under the current grazing lease, calls for early intensive stocking (EIS) of cattle and annual spring burning. This management does not fully simulate the temporal or spatial variability characteristic of a native tallgrass ecosystem, particularly the seasonality and behavior of fire. The approved TAPR General Management Plan (GMP) calls for a shift to a spatially and temporally variable fire and grazing regime. Starting in 2001, initial changes were made to decrease fire frequency and implement EIS with lighter stocking rates in the two southern pastures (Redhouse and Crusher, Table 1). However, Redhouse did receive higher than prescribed stocking in 2002, while Gashouse received less than prescribed stocking (although still more than Redhouse and Crusher) for 2001, 2002 and 2003.

Table 1. Years of prescribed burning in four pastures at TAPR.

Pasture	1997	1998	1999	2000	2001	2002	2003
Windmill	X	X	X	X	X	X	X
Gashouse	X	X	X	X	X	X	X
Redhouse	X	X	X			X	
Crusher	X	X	X	X	X		X

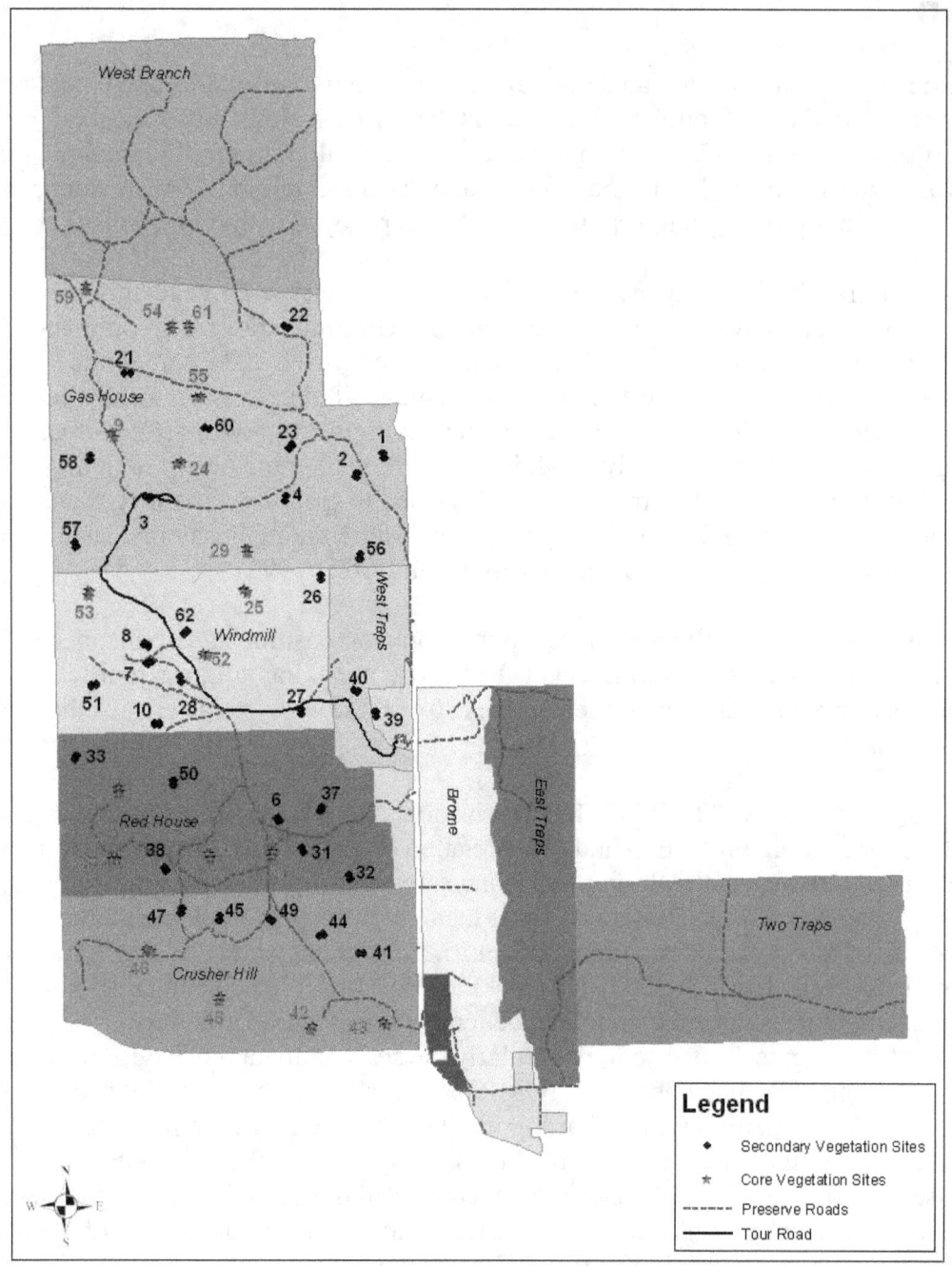

Figure 1. Map of TAPR showing pastures and HTLN core and secondary sites.

2

Methods

Field Methods

The Heartland Inventory and Monitoring Network and Prairie Cluster Prototype Monitoring Program (HTLN) implemented monitoring at TAPR in 2000 to provide analysis of baseline conditions and to assess future change in floral communities (see Willson et al. 2002 for detailed information on monitoring protocol). Forty-nine sample sites were established during the 2000-2001 period throughout four pastures at TAPR (Fig. 1). Current analysis focuses on 18 core plots that have been monitored for the last two years (2002-2003), encompassing the major soils and corresponding plant communities on TAPR. The years of 2000-2001 primarily focused on establishing permanent sample sites and the small amount of data from these years was not a focus for analysis. Secondary plots were also established to encompass the range of soils present at TAPR, but are sampled less frequently. A smaller set of data is available ranging back to 1997 for the northern two pastures (Gashouse and Windmill; Eddy 1999), which is useful for comparison of long-term trends in species groups. Data are collected each year in two sampling trips, one in late spring and one in early fall. In this way, accurate cover estimates and identification of warm season grasses and summer/fall flowering forbs can occur.

The HTLN sampling design, based on the design of the Konza Prairie Long-Term Ecological Research Program, consists of randomly located, permanent, paired transects 50 m long and 20 m apart with five circular 10 m^2 plots systematically spaced along each transect (Fig. 2). Each 10 m^2 plot also includes nested subplots of 1m^2, 0.1 m^2 and 0.01 m^2 for frequency estimates at multiple scales. Working systematically from the smallest subplot (0.01 m^2) to the largest (10 m^2), all species are identified and foliar cover is estimated.

Analytical Methods

Given the complexity of ecological drivers in the prairie ecosystem, community composition at TAPR is assessed with several metrics. Measuring foliar cover of species, calculating species frequency, richness, diversity and the exotic/native ratio are among the means used to assess community composition.

As well as analysis of individual species, plants guilds are also assessed at TAPR. Often the use of plant guilds can be a helpful analytical tool for understanding ecological patterns and processes. Generally, plant guilds are classified by shared features, such as structural morphology, photosynthetic processes, drought tolerance, and the presence of woody tissue. These features generally reflect differences in the way resources such as light, water and nutrients are obtained. Guilds simplify the array of species into groups making ecosystem processes and functions more easily understood (Kindscher 1994). The use of plant guilds can also compensate for errors related to field sampling identification.

Additionally, a species classification using response to management can be useful for analysis. John Weaver (1954) observed that prairie species respond differently to grazing and created the use of the terms "increasers and decreasers" based on the observation. Decreasers are those species that are more palatable to cattle and/or are affected by the physical presence of large ungulates and decline in abundance and size under grazing pressure. Conversely, increasers are non-palatable prairie species that increase in abundance and size under intense grazing pressure

3

due to such factors as decreased competition or change in physical environment. An abundance of increaser species could indicate possible overgrazing in the tallgrass prairie. Conversely, an abundance of decreasers could indicate overall "good" health of a prairie. This classification allows for a quick qualitative analysis of the condition of the prairie (Fraser and Kindscher 1997). Frequency and cover of 14 increaser species and 13 decreaser species was analyzed over the baseline period of 2002-2003 at TAPR.

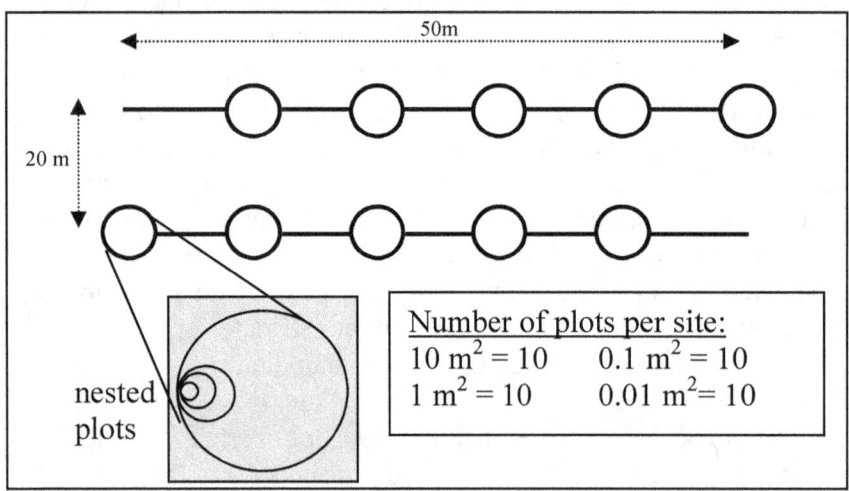

Figure 2. Vegetation community sampling design used by the Heartland network showing transects and plots including nested plots.

Analyzing patterns in species richness at both the sample site and the preserve-wide level allows three kinds of diversity to be calculated for TAPR (Whittaker 1972). Alpha diversity, local level diversity, is calculated as the average species richness per sample site, while gamma diversity, landscape level diversity, is estimated as the total number of species across all sample sites (McCune and Mefford 1997). Beta diversity, as a measure of the heterogeneity in the data, is calculated as (Whittaker 1972):

$$\beta w = (Sc \, / \, S) - 1$$

where:

        βw = beta diversity,
        Sc = the number of species in the composite sample,
        S = the average species richness in the sample units.

As a rule of thumb, values of $\beta w < 1$ are rather low and $\beta w > 5$ are considered high beta diversity (McCune and Grace 2002). If $\beta w = 0$, then all sample units have all of the species. The one is subtracted to make zero beta diversity correspond to zero variation in species presence. While this measure does not have any formal units, the result can be thought of in approximate units as the "number of distinct communities" (McCune and Grace 2002).

Results

Baseline Conditions

During the 2002-2003 sampling period, 158 unique species were found on HTLN sample sites at TAPR including 40 families. Annual richness (gamma diversity) ranged from 130 to 147 species with few exotics (Tables 2 and 3). On average, 57 species were found per sample unit (alpha diversity) resulting in an average, preserve-wide measure of beta diversity of 1.43 (Table 4). Warm season grasses such as indiangrass (*Sorghastrum nutans* (L.) Nash) and big bluestem

Table 2. Plant community composition: species richness and shannon diversity.

Measure	2002	2003	2-Year Avg. (SD)
All Species			
Richness	130	147	138.5 (12.02)
Total Diversity	2.71	3.27	2.99 (0.40)
Mean Diversity (SD)	2.39 (0.35)	2.88 (0.25)	2.64 (0.35)
Total Evenness	0.56	0.66	0.61 (0.07)
Mean Evenness (SD)	0.61 (0.08)	0.70 (0.05)	0.66 (0.06)
Native Species Only			
Richness	124	135	129.5 (7.78)
Total Diversity	2.70	3.23	2.97 (0.37)
Mean Diversity (SD)	2.38	2.86	2.62 (0.34)
Total Evenness	0.56	0.66	0.61 (0.07)
Mean Evenness (SD)	2.38	2.86	2.62 (0.34)

Table 3. Plant community composition: relative frequency and cover of exotic species.

Measure	2002	2003	2-Year Avg. (SD)
Exotic Species	5	10	7.5 (3.54)
Native Species	124	135	129.5 (7.78)
Ratio E/(E+N)	0.039	0.069	0.054 (0.02)
Exotic Species			
Relative Frequency	0.79%	2.10%	1.45% (0.93)
Relative Cover	0.21%	0.88%	0.55% (0.47)
Native Species			
Relative Frequency	99.21%	97.90%	98.55% (0.93)
Relative Cover	99.79%	99.12%	99.45% (0.47)

Table 4. Three levels of diversity for entire TAPR preserve, as well as four pastures for baselines years of 2002 and 2003.

Pasture	N	alpha		beta		gamma	
		2002	2003	2002	2003	2002	2003
Gashouse	7	49.6	61.9	0.75	0.97	87	122
Windmill	3	60.0	62.3	1.53	1.43	92	89
Redhouse	4	53.2	63.2	1.71	1.61	91	102
Crusher	4	48.5	61.5	1.79	1.77	87	109
Entire Preserve	18	51.9	62.2	1.50	1.36	130	147

(*Andropogon gerardii* Vitman) are the major components of the flora, ranging from 53 to 75% of the floral coverage within a sample site depending on the year (Tables 5 and 6). Less significant but still prominent components of the flora at TAPR include cool-season grasses such as Junegrass (*Koeleria macrantha* (Ledeb.) J.A. Schultes) and buffalo grass (*Buchloe dactyloides*

Table 5. Plant community composition: relative cover of native plant guilds.

Plant Guild	2002	2003	2-Year Avg. (SD)
Annuals/Biennials	0.87%	11.21%	6.04% (7.31)
Cool Season Grasses	5.15%	8.30%	6.73% (2.23)
Ephemeral Spring Forbs	1.48%	1.69%	1.59% (0.15)
Grass-like	1.37%	1.97%	1.67% (0.42)
Legumes	1.42%	2.99%	2.21% (1.11)
Spring Forbs	2.59%	3.35%	2.97% (0.54)
Succulents	0.05%	0.09%	0.07% (0.03)
Summer/Fall Forbs	5.89%	12.57%	9.23% (4.72)
Warm Season Grasses	75.27%	52.50%	63.89% (16.1)
Woody Shrubs and Vines	5.77%	5.06%	5.42% (0.50)

Table 6. Plant community composition: relative frequency of native plant guilds.

Plant Guild	2002	2003	2-Year Avg. (SD)
Annuals/Biennials	3.30%	14.28%	8.79% (7.76)
Cool Season Grasses	10.45%	8.79%	9.62% (1.17)
Ephemeral Spring Forbs	6.94%	6.16%	6.55% (0.55)
Grass-like	4.85%	3.63%	4.24% (0.86)
Legumes	6.47%	7.06%	6.77% (0.42)
Spring Forbs	9.85%	9.42%	9.64% (0.30)
Succulents	0.26%	0.19%	0.23% (0.05)
Summer/Fall Forbs	21.51%	20.41%	20.96% (0.78)
Warm Season Grasses	31.73%	26.11%	28.92% (3.97)
Woody Shrubs and Vines	4.05%	3.40%	3.73 (0.46)

(Nutt.) Englem.), grass-like species of sedges and rushes, woody species including dwarf prairie rose (*Rosa arkansana* Porter) and smooth sumac (*Rhus glabra* L.), showy spring forbs such as butterfly milkweed (*Asclepias tuberosa* L.), 26 species of summer and fall flowering forbs, 15 species of legumes and two cacti.

Most species guilds showed little inter-annual variation between 2002 and 2003 (Tables 5 and 6). However, two species guilds did show significant differences between 2002 and 2003. The annuals and biennials showed significantly higher frequency and cover in 2003 than 2002, while warm season grasses had lower cover in 2003 than 2002.

Exotics, most notably Kentucky bluegrass (*Poa pratensis* L.) and redseed plantain (*Plantago rhodosperma* Dcne.), comprise only a small component of the vegetation at TAPR (Table 7). Dominant species (i.e. those with high importance values) include native species such as big bluestem, little bluestem (*Schizachyrium scoparium* (Michx.) Nash), side-oats grass-grass (*Bouteloua curtipendula* (Michx.) Torr.) and lead plant (*Amorpha canescens* Pursh) (Table 8) (see Appendix for full species list). As expected, grass and grass-like species dominated the community structure with a mean cover of 46%, with very little shrub cover (4%) (Table 9). Unvegetated ground was predominantly bare soil (59%) with some grass litter (32%) (Table 10).

Table 7. Plant community composition: exotic species.

Species	Common Name	Frequency	Mean Cover	Importance Value (SD)
Plantago rhodosperma	Plantain	22.50%	0.52%	0.00425 (0.00272)
Poa pratensis	Kentucky	14.17%	1.34%	0.00385 (0.00039)
Digitaria ischaemum	Smooth crabgrass	1.95%	0.43%	0.00055 (0.00039)
Veronica arvensis	Corn speedwell	1.95%	0.25%	0.00035 (0.00025)
Stellaria media	Common	1.67%	0.46%	0.00035 (0.00025)
Lactuca serriola	Prickly lettuce	1.11%	0.25%	0.0002 (0.00014)
Lepidium campestre	Field-cress	0.56%	0.25%	0.0001 (0.00007)
Thiaspi arvense	Field penny-cress	0.56%	0.25%	0.0001 (0.00007)
Capsella bursa-pastoris	Shepherd's purse	0.56%	0.50%	0.0001 (0.00)
Setaria viridis	Green foxtail-	0.28%	0.25%	0.00005 (0.00004)
Rumex crispus	Curly dock	0.28%	0.25%	0.00005 (0.00004)
Arenaria serpyllifolia	Thyme leaf	0.28%	0.25%	0.00005 (.000004)

Table 8. Plant community composition: herbaceous and shrub species with an importance value greater than 0.02 (all species listed in Appendix).

Species	Common Name	Frequency	Mean Cover	Importance Value (SD)
Andropogon gerardii	Big bluestem	99.44%	15.25%	0.1336(0.0371)
Schizachyrium scoparium	Little bluestem	99.72%	7.34%	0.07535(0.0303)
Boufeloua curtipendula	Side-oats grama-grass	98.06%	7.37%	0.07535(0.0139)
Amorpha canescens	Lead-plant	98.06%	3.51%	0.0445(0.0051)
Buchloe dactyloides	Buffalograss	67.50%	4.51%	0.0362(0.0116)
Panicum virgatum	Switchgrass	89.45%	2.62%	0.03435(0.01)
Bouteloua hirsuta	Hairy grama-grass	58.61%	4.23%	0.0302(0.0106)
Sorgastrum nutans	Indian grass	93.06%	1.78%	0.02985(0.011)
Sporobolus asper	Tall dropseed	93.61%	1.83%	0.0298(0.0016)
Amphiachyris dracunculoides	Broomweed	43.34%	3.30%	0.0265 (0.0368)
Symphyotrichum ericoides	Squarrose white wild aster	84.72%	1.52%	0.0256 (0.0078)
Carex spp.	Sedges	97.22%	0.10%	0.0251 (0.00)
Ambrosia psilostachya	Western ragweed	90.28%	1.08%	0.02375(0.005)
Eragrostis spectabilis	Purple lovegrass	93.61%	0.83%	0.0231 (0.0023)
Vernonia baldwinii	Western ironweed	76.95%	1.37%	0.0225 (0.0035)
Bouteloua gracilis	Blue grama	36.39%	5.69%	0.02125(0.0043)
Dichanthelium spp.	Panic grasses	92.22%	0.59%	0.02115(0.0036)

Table 9. Plant community structure: mean percent cover for the shrub and herbaceous layers.

Plant Type	2002	2003	2-Year Avg. (SD)
Grasses/Grass-like	52.85	40.09	46.47 (9.02)
Herbs	7.47	20.05	13.76 (8.90)
Shrubs	4.10	3.49	3.80 (0.43)

Table 10. Plant community structure: mean percent cover for the ground layer.

Structural Component	2002	2003	2-Year Avg. (SD)
Bare Soil	59.11	58.10	58.61 (0.71)
Bare Rock	9.24	11.61	10.43 (1.68)
Grass Litter	37.72	26.94	32.33 (7.62)
Woody Debris	0.04	0.07	0.06 (0.02)
Leaf Litter	0.04	0.07	0.06 (0.02)
Unvegetated Surface	86.81	86.04	86.43 (0.54)

As a qualitative measure of prairie health, the frequency and abundance of increaser and decreaser species, as defined by Fraser and Kindscher (1997) was inconclusive. Certain forb species commonly associated with heavy grazing (i.e. western ironweed, *Vernonia baldwinii* Torr. and white heath aster, *Symphyotrichum ericoides* (L.) Nesom) occur at conspicuously high frequencies in the prairie. On the other hand, other species classified as increasers such as clammy ground cherry (*Physalis heterophylla* Nees) and hoary verbena (*Verbena stricta* Vent.) are present only negligibly (Table 11).

Table 11. Average frequency and cover of plant species classified by Fraser and Kindscher (1997) as increasing or decreasing with intensive grazing pressure.

Scientific Name	Common Name	Grazing	Average Frequency (%)		Average Cover (%)	
			2002	2003	2002	2003
Amorpha canescens	leadplant	decreaser	97.78	98.33	3.85	3.16
Andropogon gerardii	big bluestem	decreaser	99.44	99.44	18.81	11.67
Aster sericeus	western silvery wild	decreaser	7.22	8.33	0.11	0.15
Astragalus	ground plum, prairie	decreaser	5.00	10.56	0.14	0.28
Comandra umbellata	bastard toad-flax	decreaser	0.56	0.56	0.03	0.03
Dalea candida	white prairie clover	decreaser	1.67	3.33	0.08	0.11
Dalea purpurea	purple prairie clover	decreaser	46.11	47.22	0.42	0.36
Elymus canadensis	Canada wild rye	decreaser	3.33	5.00	0.11	0.11
Panicum virgatum	switchgrass	decreaser	83.33	95.56	1.58	3.33
Psoratea esculenfa	bread root scurf-pea	decreaser	7.78	18.33	0.19	0.33
Rosa arkansana	dwarf prairie rose	decreaser	1.67	1.67	0.06	0.06
Sisyrinchium	blue-eyed grass	decreaser	25.56	32.78	0.39	0.47
Viola pedatifida	prairie violet	decreaser	22.78	21.67	0.28	0.28
Achillea millefolium	common yarrow	increaser	28.33	28.89	0.47	0.42
Antennaria neglecta	field pussytoes	increaser	22.22	26.67	0.50	0.65
Artemisia ludoviciana	white sage	increaser	37.78	33.89	0.75	0.71
Asclepia verticillata	whorled milkweed	increaser	13.89	16.11	0.31	0.31
Symphyotrichum	white heath aster	increaser	82.22	87.22	0.57	2.30
Baptisia bracteata v. leucophaea	plains wild indigo	increaser	6.67	13.89	0.24	0.97
Buchloe dactyloides	buffalograss	increaser	61.11	73.89	2.66	4.90
Eragrostis spectabilis	purple lovegrass	increaser	92.78	94.44	0.83	0.81
Erigeron strigosus	rough fleabane	increaser	7.22	1.67	0.08	0.08
Physalis heterophylla	clammy ground cherry	increaser	0.00	1.11	0.00	0.06
Poa pratensis	Kentucky bluegrass	increaser	12.78	15.56	0.21	0.45
Solidago missouriensis	Missouri goldenrod	increaser	9.44	45.00	0.31	0.52
Verbena stricta	hoary verbena	increaser	7.78	9.44	0.17	0.22
Vermonia baldwinii	western ironweed	increaser	75.56	78.33	0.79	1.75

Preliminary Trend Detection

Given differences in sample effort since 1997 and the evolution of taxonomic knowledge, it is not yet possible to comment on trends in the effect of management activity at TAPR since 1997 on individual species. However, it is possible to examine general trends in the abundance of groups of species, since they are less affected by sampling error. Since 1997, cover of warm season grasses has varied significantly year to year, perhaps due to weather (Fig. 3). Meanwhile, cool-season grasses have shown a steady increase (Fig. 3), while annuals/biennials had high abundance in 2001 and 2003. The annual species broomweed (*Amphiachyris dracunculoides* (DC.) Nutt.) was seen in vast abundance in both 2001 and 2003 (Fig. 4).

Preliminary Comparison of Management Regimes

Preliminary changes to fire return intervals and stocking rates have not resulted in significant differences between pastures for the metrics measured. Preliminary results indicate that Redhouse, with reduced fire and stocking, had a slightly greater increase in annuals and biennials in 2003 than Windmill, but less of an increase in summer forbs than Windmill and Crusher (Fig. 5). Research at Konza Prairie LTER Program also found increased forb cover with increased fire frequency in grazed prairie (Knapp et al. 1998). It may be too early to see significant changes in plant guilds caused by initial changes in fire frequency in Crusher and Redhouse pastures. The pastures with reduced fire and stocking showed decreases in beta diversity from 2002 to 2003, as did Windmill pasture (Table 3). Gashouse was the only pasture to show increased beta diversity.

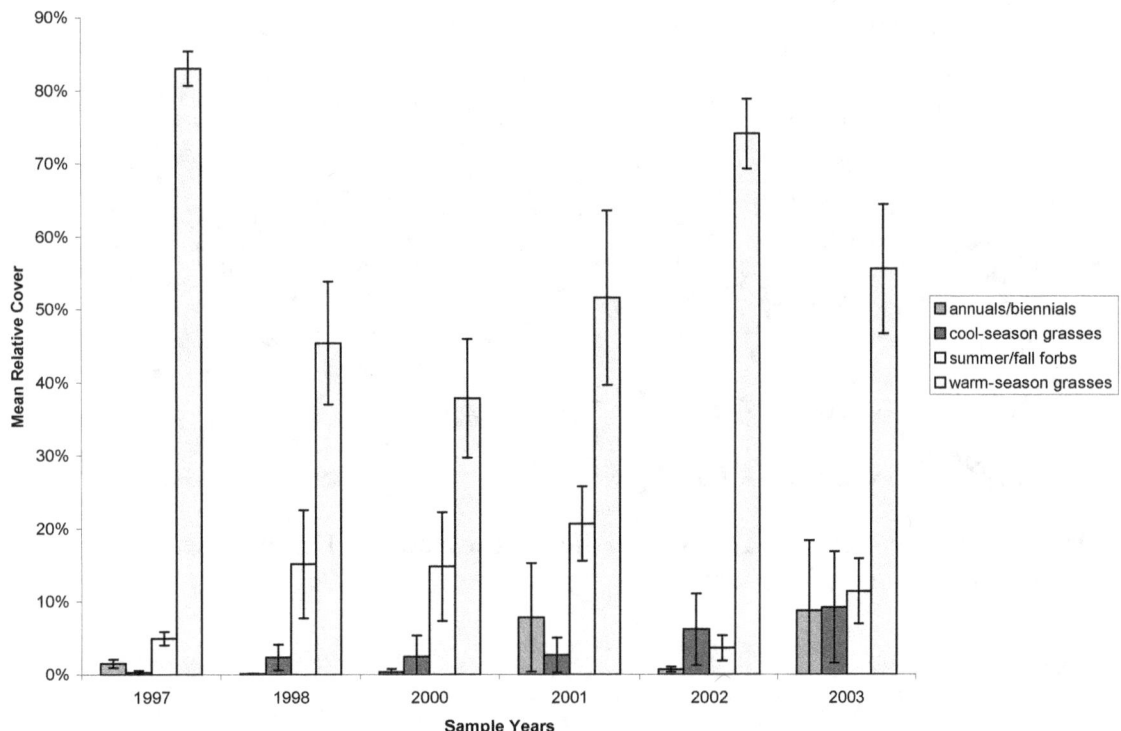

Figure 3. Average guild abundance over entire sampling period at TAPR for northern two pastures (Windmill and Gashouse).

Figure 4. October 2003 landscape at TAPR showing yellow patches of broomweed, *Amphiachyris dracunculoides* (DC.) Nutt.

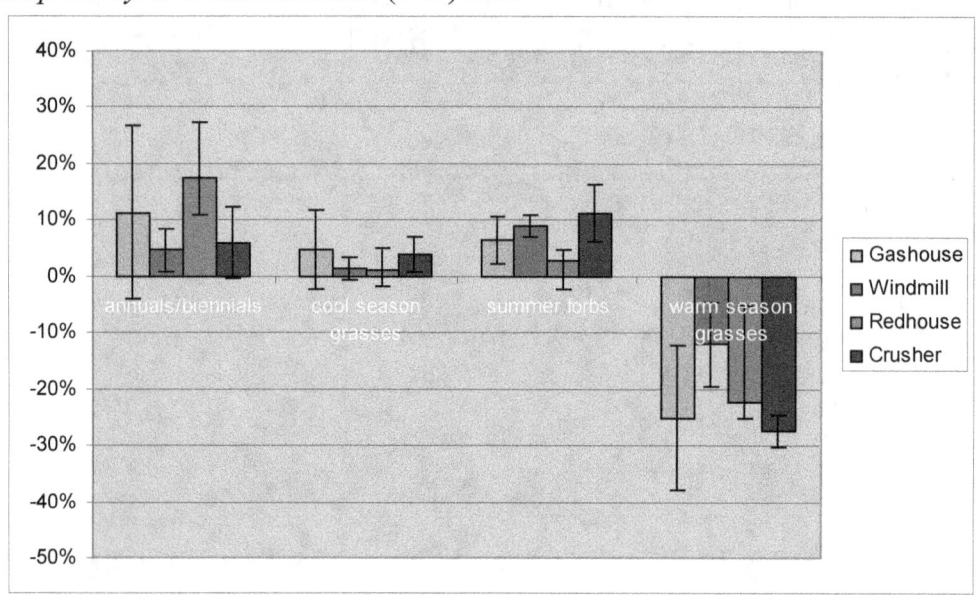

Figure 5. Percent change in abundance of plant guilds for each pasture 2002 to 2003.

Discussion

Early intensive grazing and annual spring burning, implemented in the last 20+ years, has had an overall homogenizing effect on the landscape. This is reflected by the low beta diversity seen preserve-wide. Alternate management, such as reduced stocking and a variable fire regime, may increase beta diversity. So far, the minor modifications to the stocking rate (except Windmill pasture) and the fire frequency (Redhouse and Crusher pastures only) have not improved heterogeneity across the preserve.

While possibly increasing landscape heterogeneity, longer fire return intervals can also allow more annuals/biennials to become established and potentially increase invasive and exotic species previously controlled by frequent fire. While annuals and biennials have increased at TAPR, especially in Redhouse, exotics are still relatively absent. As heterogeneity of fire and grazing increases at TAPR, existing exotics could increase in frequency or abundance. Additionally, while the use of grazing indicator species (Fraser and Kindscher 1997) was inconclusive as a means of quickly assessing the health of the prairie, increasers and decreasers will continue to be monitored in the future as management changes.

In addition to grazing and fire, climatic variability is an important factor driving plant community dynamics at TAPR, with species responding to variability in annual precipitation. Precipitation in 2003 is the first since 1999 to be above the 30-year average (Fig. 6). Increases in annuals/biennials occurred in 2001 and 2003, most notably broomweed. Towne and Owensby (1983) found that increased bare ground resulting from a combination of drought, grazing, mowing and/or fire significantly increased the amount of broomweed in the Kansas Flint Hills. At TAPR, significant increases in broomweed occurred preserve-wide without regard to management regimes. Photopoint interpretation has also captured a negative effect of low precipitation levels on perennial forbs at TAPR (Barnard 2003).

It is still too early to determine the effects of changes in cattle stocking and fire frequencies on the warm season grass component of TAPR. Year-to-year and within-year changes in abundance make short-term detection of management effects on warm season grasses difficult. Future work, including better estimates of frequency for warm season grasses through ancillary sampling, will likely increase knowledge of changes in abundance of plant guilds and the effects of change in management regimes. Future monitoring results when compared to the baseline period should provide a good measure of future management.

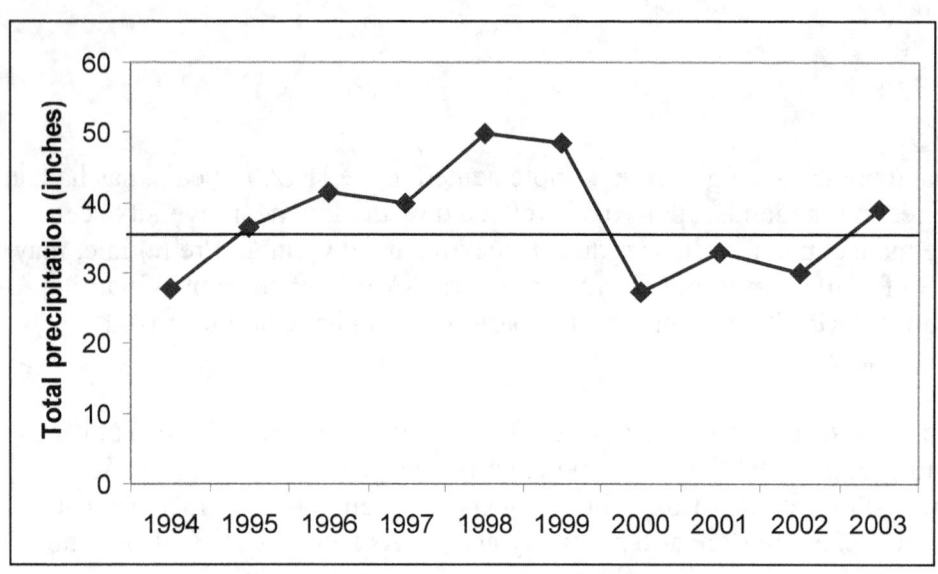

Figure 6. Thirty year averages for precipitation at TAPR 1994 to 2003. (Weather data acquired from Missouri State Climatologist for weather station ID 148061 located at TAPR.)

Literature Cited

Albertson, F. W., G. W. Tomanek and A. Riegel. 1957. Ecology of drought cycles and grazing intensity on grasslands of central Great Plains. Ecological Monographs **27**:27-44.

Axelrod, D. I. 1985. Rise of the grassland biome, central North America. Bot. Rev. **51**:163-202.

Barnard, I. 2003. Fixed point repeat photography resource monitoring on Tallgrass Prairie National Preserve. National Park Service unpublished report.

Bragg, T.B. 1995. The physical environment of Great Plains grasslands. Pages 49-81 *in* A. Joern and K. H. Keeler, editors. The Changing Prairie. Oxford University Press.

Collins, S. L. and S. M. Glenn. 1995. Grassland dynamics and landscape dynamics. Pages 128-156 *in* A. Joern and K. H. Keeler, editors. The Changing Prairie. Oxford University Press.

Collins, S. L. and S. M. Glenn. 1988. Disturbance and community structure in North America prairies. Pages 131-143 *in* H. J. During, J. A. Werger, and J. H. Willems, editors. Diversity and pattern in plant communities. SPB Academic Publication, The Hague.

Eddy, T. 1999. Prairie community summary of 1997 and 1998 vegetation sampling on the Tallgrass Prairie National Preserve. National Park Service unpublished report.

Fraser, A., and K. Kindscher. 1997. Plant species provide key to range management success. Rural Papers.

National Park Service (NPS). 2000. General Management Plan/Environmental Impact Statement, Tallgrass Prairie National Preserve, Kansas. National Park Service, Omaha, NE.

Hartnett, D. C., K. R. Hickman, and L. E. Fischer Walter. 1996. Effects of bison grazing, fire, and topography on floristic diversity in tallgrass prairie. Journal of Range Management **49**:413-420.

Hiebert, R. D. (editor). 1998. Opportunities to enhance and maintain the tallgrass prairie ecosystem within the boundaries of Tallgrass Prairie National Preserve. National Park Service, Midwest Region, Omaha, NE.

Hitchcock, A. S. 1950. Manual of the grasses of the United States. USDA Misc. Publ. No. 200. Washington, DC.

Kindscher, K. 1994. Rockefeller Prairie: A case study on the use of plant guild classification of a tallgrass prairie. Pages 123-124 *in* R. G. Wickett, P. N. Lewis, A. Woodliffe, and P. Pratt, editors. Proceedings of the Thirteenth Annual North American Prairie Conference.

Knapp, A. K., J. M. Briggs, D. C. Hartnett, and S. L. Collins (editors). 1998. Grassland dynamics: long-term ecological research in tallgrass prairie. Oxford University Press.

Knapp, A. K., J. M. Briggs, D. C. Hartnett, and D. W. Kaufman. 1993. Long term ecological research at the Konza Prairie Research Natural Area: Site description and research summary (1981-1992). Division of Biology, Kansas State University, Manhattan, KS.

McCune, B., and J. B. Grace. 2002. Analysis of ecological communities. MjM Software Design, Gleneden Beach, Oregon.

McCune, B., and M. J. Mefford. 1997. PC-ORD. Multivariate Analysis of Ecological Data. Version 3.0. MjM Software, Gleneden Beach, Oregon.

Plumb, G. E., and J. L. Dodd. 1993. Foraging ecology of bison and cattle on a mixed prairie: Implications for natural area management. Ecological Applications **3**:631-643.

Towne, G., and C. E. Owensby. 1983. Annual broomweed [Gutierrezia dracunculoides (DC.) Blake] response to burning and mulch addition. Journal of Range Management **36**:711-712.

Weaver, J. E. 1943. Replacement of true prairie by mixed prairie in eastern Nebraska and Kansas. Ecology **24**:421-434.

Weaver, J. E. 1954. North American Prairie. Johnsen Publishing Company, Lincoln NE.

Whittaker, R. H. 1972. Evolution and measurement of species diversity. Taxon **21**:213-251.

Willson, G. D., L. P. Thomas, M. DeBacker, W. M. Rizzo, and C. Buck. 2002. Plant community monitoring protocol for six prairie parks. U.S. Department of the Interior, U.S. Geological Survey.

Appendix. Species list for Tallgrass Prairie National Preserve including years 1997 to 2003.

Guilds: annual-biennial = opportunistic herbaceous species that complete life cycle in one or two years; coolgrass = cool season grass, members of Poaceae, initiate flowering prior to July; ephemeral = herbaceous spring forbs characterized by short flowering period in spring (typically in late March or April), foliage dries up by early summer; grass-like = species which resemble grasses in their growth form and morphology, terrestrial members of Juncaceae and Cyperaceae; legume = members of Fabaceae, capable of fixing nitrogen through root nodules; spring forb = herbaceous species that initiate flowering prior to June, but persist through summer months; summer/fall forb = herbaceous, initiate flowering in or after July; warmgrass = warm season grass, members of Poaceae, flowering in or after July; woody = perennial species with over wintering aboveground structures, includes trees, shrubs and woody vines; succulents = perennial succulent herbs, shrubs and small trees.

Scientific name	Common Name	Family	Guild
Acalypha ostryifolia	Pineland threeseed mecury	Euphorbiaceae	annual-biennial
Acalypha virginica	Virginia threeseed mecury	Euphorbiaceae	annual-biennial
Achillea millefolium	Common yarrow	Asteraceae	ephemeral
Agalinis aspera	Tall false foxglove	Scrophulariaceae	annual-biennial
Agalinis tenuifolia	Slenderleaf false foxglove	Scrophulariaceae	annual-biennial
Ageratina altissima	White snakeroot	Asteraceae	summer/fall forb
Agrostis hyemalis	Winter bentgrass	Poaceae	coolgrass
Alliaria petiolata	Garlic-mustard	Brassicaceae	annual-biennial
Allium canadense	Meadow garlic	Liliaceae	spring forb
Alopecurus carolinianus	Carolina foxtail	Poaceae	coolgrass
Ambrosia psilostachya	Cuman ragweed	Asteraceae	summer/fall forb
Ambrosia trifida	Great ragweed	Asteraceae	annual-biennial
Amorpha canescens	Lead-plant	Fabaceae	woody
Amphiachyris dracunculoides	Prairie broomweed	Asteraceae	annual-biennial
Andropogon gerardii	Big bluestem	Poaceae	warmgrass
Androsace occidentalis	Western rockjasmine	Primulaceae	annual-biennial
Antennaria neglecta	Field pussytoes	Asteraceae	spring forb
Apocynum cannabinum	Indianhemp	Apocynaceae	spring forb

Scientific name	Common Name	Family	Guild
Arctium minus	Lesser burdock	Asteraceae	annual-biennial
Arenaria serpyllifolia	Thyme leaf sandwort	Caryophyllaceae	annual-biennial
Aristida oligantha	Prairie three-awn	Poaceae	warmgrass
Artemisia ludoviciana	White sagebrush	Asteraceae	summer/fall forb
Asclepias stenophylla	Slimleaf milkweed	Asclepiadaceae	summer/fall forb
Asclepias syriaca	Common milkweed	Asclepiadaceae	spring forb
Asclepias tuberosa	Butterfly-milkweed	Asclepiadaceae	spring forb
Asclepias verticillata	Whorled milkweed	Asclepiadaceae	spring forb
Asclepias viridiflora	Greencomet milkweed	Asclepiadaceae	summer/fall forb
Asclepias viridis	Green antelopehorn	Asclepiadaceae	spring forb
Aster drummondii	Drummond's aster	Asteraceae	summer/fall forb
Aster ericoides	White heath aster	Asteraceae	summer/fall forb
Aster laevis	Smooth blue aster	Asteraceae	summer/fall forb
Aster oblongifolius	Aromatic aster	Asteraceae	summer/fall forb
Aster sericeus	Western silvery aster	Asteraceae	summer/fall forb
Astragalus canadensis	Canada milk-vetch	Fabaceae	legume
Astragalus crassicarpus	Ground-plum, prairie plum milk-vetch	Fabaceae	legume
Astragalus lotiflorus	Lotus milk-vetch	Fabaceae	legume
Baptisia australis	Blue wild indigo	Fabaceae	legume
Baptisia bracteata var. leucophaea	Long bract wild indigo	Fabaceae	legume
Bouteloua curtipendula	Side-oats grama-grass	Poaceae	warmgrass
Bouteloua gracilis	Blue grama	Poaceae	warmgrass
Bouteloua hirsuta	Hairy grama-grass	Poaceae	warmgrass
Brickellia eupatorioides	False boneset	Asteraceae	summer/fall forb
Buchloe dactyloides	Buffalograss	Poaceae	coolgrass
Cacalia plantaginea	Groovestem Indian plantain	Asteraceae	summer/fall forb
Callirhoe alcaeoides	Light poppy-mallow	Malvaceae	ephemeral
Calylophus serrulatus	Yellow sundrops	Onagraceae	spring forb
Capsella bursa-pastoris	Shepherd's purse	Brassicaceae	annual-biennial
Carex amphibola	Eastern narrowleaf sedge	Cyperaceae	grass-like

Scientific name	Common Name	Family	Guild
Carex blanda	Eastern woodland sedge	Cyperaceae	grass-like
Carex brevior	Shortbeak sedge	Cyperaceae	grass-like
Carex meadii	Mead's sedge	Cyperaceae	grass-like
Ceanothus americanus	New Jersey tea, redroot	Rhamnaceae	woody
Ceanothus herbaceus	Jersey tea	Rhamnaceae	woody
Cerastium brachypodum	Short-stalk chickweed	Caryophyllaceae	Perennial
Chaerophyllum procumbens	Spreading chervil	Apiaceae	annual-biennial
Chamaesyce prostrata	Prostrate sandmat	Euphorbiaceae	annual-biennial
Chenopodium album	Lamb's quarters, pigweed	Chenopodiaceae	annual-biennial
Chenopodium berlandieri	Pitseed goosefoot	Chenopodiaceae	annual-biennial
Chloris verticillata	Tumble windmill grass	Poaceae	coolgrass
Cirsium altissimum	Tall thistle	Asteraceae	annual-biennial
Cirsium undulatum	Wavy-leaved thistle	Asteraceae	summer/fall forb
Clematis terniflora	Sweet autumn virgin's bower	Ranunculaceae	woody
Comandra umbellata	Bastard toad-flax	Santalaceae	spring forb
Convolvulus arvensis	Field-bindweed	Convolvulaceae	summer/fall forb
Conyza canadensis	Canadian horseweed	Asteraceae	annual-biennial
Cornus drummondii	Rough-leaved dogwood	Cornaceae	woody
Corydalis micrantha	Small flower fumewort	Fumariaceae	annual-biennial
Croton capitatus	Hogwort	Euphorbiaceae	annual-biennial
Croton monanthogynus	Prairie-tea	Euphorbiaceae	annual-biennial
Cynanchum laeve	Honey vine	Asclepiadaceae	summer/fall forb
Cyperus esculentus	Chufa flatsedge	Cyperaceae	grass-like
Dalea aurea	Golden prairie clover	Fabaceae	legume
Dalea candida	White prairie clover	Fabaceae	legume
Dalea multiflora	Roundhead prairie clover	Fabaceae	legume
Dalea purpurea	Violet prairie clover	Fabaceae	legume
Delphinium carolinianum	Carolina larkspur	Ranunculaceae	spring forb
Delphinium carolinianum ssp. Virescens	Carolina larkspur	Ranunculaceae	spring forb
Descurainia pinnata	Western tansy-mustard	Brassicaceae	annual-biennial

Scientific name	Common Name	Family	Guild
Desmanthus illinoensis	Prairie bundleflower	Fabaceae	legume
Desmodium cuspidatum	Large bract tick-trefoil	Fabaceae	legume
Desmodium illinoense	Illinois tick-trefoil	Fabaceae	legume
Dichanthelium oligosanthes	Heller's rosettegrass	Poaceae	coolgrass
Digitaria cognata	Carolina crab grass	Poaceae	coolgrass
Draba brachycarpa	Shortpod draba	Brassicaceae	annual-biennial
Draba cuneifolia	Wedgeleaf draba	Brassicaceae	annual-biennial
Draba reptans	Carolina draba	Brassicaceae	annual-biennial
Echinacea angustifolia	Blacksamson coneflower	Asteraceae	summer/fall forb
Eleocharis compressa	Flat-stem spike-rush	Cyperaceae	grass-like
Ellisia nyctelea	Aunt Lucy	Hydrophyllaceae	annual-biennial
Elymus canadensis	Canada wild rye	Poaceae	coolgrass
Eragrostis spectabilis	Purple lovegrass	Poaceae	warmgrass
Erigeron philadelphicus	Philadelphia f;leabane	Asteraceae	ephemeral
Erigeron strigosus	Prairie fleabane	Asteraceae	annual-biennial
Erythronium mesochoreum	Midland fawnlily	Liliaceae	ephemeral
Escobaria missouriensis var. Missouriensis	Missouri foxtail cactus	Cactaceae	succulent
Eupatorium altissimum	Tall thoroughwort	Asteraceae	summer/fall forb
Euphorbia corollata	Flowering spurge	Euphorbiaceae	summer/fall forb
Euphorbia dentata	Toothed spurge	Euphorbiaceae	annual-biennial
Euphorbia marginata	Snow-on-the-mountain	Euphorbiaceae	annual-biennial
Euphorbia spathulata	Warty spurge	Euphorbiaceae	annual-biennial
Euthamia gymnospermoides	Texas goldenrod	Asteraceae	summer/fall forb
Evolvulus nuttallianus	Shaggy dwarf morning-glory	Convolvulaceae	spring forb
Festuca subverticillata	Nodding fescue	Poaceae	coolgrass
Galium aparine	Stickywilly	Rubiaceae	annual-biennial
Galium circaezans	Licorice bedstraw	Rubiaceae	spring forb
Geranium carolinianum	Bricknell's crane's-bill	Geraniaceae	annual-biennial
Geum canadense	White avens	Rosaceae	spring forb
Grindelia squarrosa	Curly-top gum-weed	Asteraceae	annual-biennial

Scientific name	Common Name	Family	Guild
Hedeoma hispida	Rough false pennyroyal	Lamiaceae	annual-biennial
Hedyotis nigricans var. Nigricans	Diamondflowers	Rubiaceae	spring forb
Helianthus maximiliani	Maximilian sunflower	Asteraceae	summer/fall forb
Hieracium longipilum	Hairy hawkweed	Asteraceae	summer/fall forb
Hordeum pusillum	Little barley	Poaceae	coolgrass
Hybanthus verticillatus	Baby slippers	Violaceae	ephemeral
Hymenopappus scabiosaeus	Carolina woollywhite	Asteraceae	spring forb
Juncus interior	Inland rush	Juncaceae	grass-like
Kochia scoparia	Mexican fireweed	Chenopodiaceae	annual-biennial
Koeleria macrantha	Junegrass	Poaceae	coolgrass
Krigia cespitosa	Weedy dwarfdandelion	Asteraceae	annual-biennial
Kummerowia stipulacea	Korean clover	Fabaceae	legume
Lactuca serriola	Prickly lettuce	Asteraceae	annual-biennial
Lamium amplexicaule	Henbit dead nettle	Lamiaceae	annual-biennial
Laportea canadensis	Canadian woodnettle	Urticaceae	summer/fall forb
Leersia oryziodes	Rice cut-grass	Poaceae	warmgrass
Lepidium campestre	Field pepper weed	Brassicaceae	annual-biennial
Lepidium densiflorum	Common pepperweed	Brassicaceae	annual-biennial
Lespedeza capitata	Bush-clover	Fabaceae	legume
Lespedeza violacea	Violet lespedeza	Fabaceae	legume
Lespedeza virginica	Slender lespedeza	Fabaceae	legume
Liatris aspera	Tall blazing star	Asteraceae	summer/fall forb
Liatris punctata	Dotted blazing star, gay feather	Asteraceae	summer/fall forb
Linum sulcatum	Grooved flax	Linaceae	annual-biennial
Lithospermum incisum	Narrow-leaved stoneseed	Boraginaceae	spring forb
Lobelia cardinalis	Cardinal-flower	Campanulaceae	summer/fall forb
Lomatium foeniculaceum	Desert biscuitroot	Apiaceae	ephemeral
Malvastrum hispidum	Hispid false-mallow	Malvaceae	annual-biennial
Melilotus officinalis	Yellow sweet clover	Fabaceae	legume
Menispermum canadense	Common moonseed	Menispermaceae	woody

Scientific name	Common Name	Family	Guild
Mirabilis nyctaginea	Heart-leaf four o'clock	Nyctaginaceae	spring forb
Monarda fistulosa	Wild bergamot	Lamiaceae	summer/fall forb
Muhlenbergia cuspidata	Plains muhly	Poaceae	coolgrass
Muhlenbergia frondosa	Wirestem muhly	Poaceae	warmgrass
Myosotis verna	Spring forget-me-not	Boraginaceae	annual-biennial
Nothoscordum bivalve	Crowpoison	Liliaceae	ephemeral
Oenothera biennis	Common evening-primrose	Onagraceae	summer/fall forb
Oenothera macrocarpa	Big-fruit evening-primrose	Onagraceae	spring forb
Oenothera speciosa	Pink ladies	Onagraceae	spring forb
Onosmodium molle	Soft hair marbleseed	Boraginaceae	spring forb
Opuntia macrorhiza	Twistspine prickly pear	Cactaceae	succulent
Oxalis dillenii	Tufted yellow wood-sorrel	Oxalidaceae	spring forb
Oxalis violacea	Violet wood-sorrel	Oxalidaceae	spring forb
Panicum capillare	Witch-grass	Poaceae	warmgrass
Panicum virgatum	Switchgrass	Poaceae	warmgrass
Parthenocissus quinquefolia	Virginia-creeper, woodbine	Vitaceae	woody
Pascopyrum smithii	Western wheatgrass	Poaceae	coolgrass
Paspalum laeve	Field paspalum	Poaceae	warmgrass
Penstemon cobaea	Cobaea beardtongue	Scrophulariaceae	ephemeral
Penstemon tubiflorus	White-wand beard-tongue	Scrophulariaceae	spring forb
Phlox divaricata	Wild blue phlox	Polemoniaceae	spring forb
Physalis heterophylla	Clammy ground cherry	Solanaceae	spring forb
Physalis longifolia	Longleaf ground cherry	Solanaceae	spring forb
Physalis pumila	Dwarf ground cherry	Solanaceae	spring forb
Physalis virginiana	Virginia ground cherry	Solanaceae	spring forb
Phytolacca americana	American pokeweed, pokeberry	Phytolaccaceae	summer/fall forb
Plantago patagonica	Wooly plantain	Plantaginaceae	annual-biennial
Plantago pusilla	Dwarf plantain	Plantaginaceae	spring forb
Plantago rhodosperma	Redseed plantain	Plantaginaceae	annual-biennial
Plantago rugelii	Blackseed plantain	Plantaginaceae	spring forb

Scientific name	Common Name	Family	Guild
Poa arida	Plains bluegrass	Poaceae	coolgrass
Poa pratensis	Kentucky bluegrass	Poaceae	coolgrass
Polygala verticillata	Whorled milkwort	Polygalaceae	annual-biennial
Polygonum virginianum	Jumpseed	Polygonaceae	summer/fall forb
Psoralea argophylla	Silverleaf Indian breadroot	Fabaceae	legume
Psoralea esculenta	Large Indian breadrood	Fabaceae	legume
Psoralidium tenuiflorum	Slim-flower scurf-pea	Fabaceae	legume
Ratibida columnifera	Upright coneflower	Asteraceae	summer/fall forb
Rhus glabra	Smooth sumac	Anacardiaceae	woody
Ribes missouriense	Missouri gooseberry	Grossulariaceae	woody
Rosa arkansana	Prairie rose	Rosaceae	woody
Ruellia humilis	Fringeleaf wild petunia	Acanthaceae	summer/fall forb
Ruellia strepens	Limestone wild petunia	Acanthaceae	summer/fall forb
Rumex crispus	Curly dock	Polygonaceae	spring forb
Salvia azurea	Azure blue sage	Lamiaceae	summer/fall forb
Sambucus canadensis	Common elderberry	Caprifoliaceae	woody
Schizachyrium scoparium	Little bluestem	Poaceae	warmgrass
Schrankia nuttallii	Nuttallii sensitive brier	Fabaceae	legume
Scutellaria parvula	Small skullcap	Lamiaceae	spring forb
Senecio plattensis	Platte groundsel	Asteraceae	summer/fall forb
Setaria viridis	Green bristlegrass	Poaceae	warmgrass
Sida spinosa	Prickly fanpetals	Malvaceae	annual-biennial
Silene antirrhina	Sleepy silene	Caryophyllaceae	annual-biennial
Silphium laciniatum	Compass-plant	Asteraceae	summer/fall forb
Sisyrinchium campestre	Prairie blue-eyed grass	Iridaceae	ephemeral
Smilax tamnoides	Bristly greenbrier	Smilacaceae	woody
Solanum carolinense	Carolina horse-nettle	Solanaceae	spring forb
Solanum rostratum	Buffalo-bur night-shade	Solanaceae	annual-biennial
Solidago canadensis	Canada goldenrod	Asteraceae	summer/fall forb
Solidago canadensis var. Gilvocanescens	Shorthair goldenrod	Asteraceae	summer/fall forb
Solidago missouriensis	Missouri goldenrod	Asteraceae	summer/fall forb

Scientific name	Common Name	Family	Guild
Solidago rigida	Stiff goldenrod	Asteraceae	summer/fall forb
Sorghastrum nutans	Indian grass	Poaceae	warmgrass
Spermolepis inermis	Red river scaleseed	Apiaceae	annual-biennial
Spiranthes cernua	Nodding ladies' tresses	Orchidaceae	summer/fall forb
Sporobolus asper	Rough dropseed	Poaceae	warmgrass
Sporobolus neglectus	Puffsheath dropseed	Poaceae	warmgrass
Stellaria media	Common chickweed	Caryophyllaceae	annual-biennial
Strophostyles leiosperma	Silkseed fuzzy bean	Fabaceae	legume
Symphoricarpos orbiculatus	Coralberry	Caprifoliaceae	woody
Taraxacum officinale	Common dandelion	Asteraceae	spring forb
Teucrium canadense	Canada germander	Lamiaceae	summer/fall forb
Thlaspi arvense	Field penny-cress	Brassicaceae	annual-biennial
Toxicodendron radicans	Eastern poison-ivy	Anacardiaceae	woody
Tradescantia bracteata	Longbract spiderwort	Commelinaceae	spring forb
Tradescantia ohiensis	Bluejacket spiderwort	Commelinaceae	spring forb
Trichostema brachiatum	Fluxweed	Lamiaceae	annual-biennial
Tridens flavus	Purpletop tridens	Poaceae	warmgrass
Triodanis leptocarpa	Slimpod venus' looking glass	Campanulaceae	annual-biennial
Triodanis perfoliata	Clasping venus' looking glass	Campanulaceae	annual-biennial
Urtica dioica ssp. Gracilis	California nettle, stinging nettle	Urticaceae	summer/fall forb
Verbena simplex	Narrow-leaved vervain	Verbenaceae	spring forb
Verbena stricta	Hoary vervain	Verbenaceae	spring forb
Verbesina alternifolia	Wingstem	Asteraceae	summer/fall forb
Vernonia baldwinii	Baldwin's ironweed	Asteraceae	summer/fall forb
Veronica arvensis	Corn speedwell	Scrophulariaceae	annual-biennial
Veronica peregrina	Neckweed	Scrophulariaceae	annual-biennial
Viola bicolor	Field pansy	Violaceae	annual-biennial
Viola pedatifida	Prairie violet	Violaceae	spring forb

Scientific name	Common Name	Family	Guild
Viola pratincola	Northern bog violet	Violaceae	ephemeral
Viola sororia	Common blue violet	Violaceae	spring forb
Vitis riparia	Riverbank grape	Vitaceae	woody
Vulpia octoflora	Six-weeks fescue	Poaceae	coolgrass
Xanthium strumarium	Rough cocklebur	Asteraceae	annual-biennial
Zanthoxylum americanum	Common prickly ash	Rutaceae	woody
Zigadenus elegans	Mountain death camas	Liliaceae	summer/fall forb
Zigadenus nuttallii	Nuttall's deathcamas	Liliaceae	spring forb
Zizia aurea	Golden zizia	Apiaceae	spring forb

The NPS has organized its parks with significant natural resources into 32 networks linked by geography and shared natural resource characteristics. HTLN is composed of 15 National Park Service (NPS) units in eight Midwestern states. These parks contain a wide variety of natural and cultural resources including sites focused on commemorating civil war battlefields, Native American heritage, westward expansion, and our U.S. Presidents. The Network is charged with creating inventories of its species and natural features as well as monitoring trends and issues in order to make sound management decisions. Critical inventories help park managers understand the natural resources in their care while monitoring programs help them understand meaningful change in natural systems and to respond accordingly. The Heartland Network helps to link natural and cultural resources by protecting the habitat of our history.

The I&M program bridges the gap between science and management with a third of its efforts aimed at making information accessible. Each network of parks, such as Heartland, has its own multi-disciplinary team of scientists, support personnel, and seasonal field technicians whose system of online databases and reports make information and research results available to all. Greater efficiency is achieved through shared staff and funding as these core groups of professionals augment work done by individual park staff. Through this type of integration and partnership, network parks are able to accomplish more than a single park could on its own.

The mission of the Heartland Network is to collaboratively develop and conduct scientifically credible inventories and long-term monitoring of park "vital signs" and to distribute this information for use by park staff, partners, and the public, thus enhancing understanding which leads to sound decision making in the preservation of natural resources and cultural history held in trust by the National Park Service.

www.nature.nps.gov/im/units/htln/

Natural Resource Monitoring

The Department of the Interior protects and manages the nation's natural resources and cultural heritage; provides scientific and other information about those resources; and honors its special responsibilities to American Indians, Alaska Natives, and affiliated Island Communities.

NPS D-33, April 2006

Natural Resource Program Center
1201 Oakridge Drive, Suite 150
Fort Collins, CO 80525

www.nps.gov

www.ingramcontent.com/pod-product-compliance
Lightning Source LLC
Chambersburg PA
CBHW080936290526
45795CB00007BA/2778